DEPENDING ON

Also by John Mole:

Poetry

The Love Horse
A Partial Light
Our Ship
From the House Opposite
Feeding the Lake
In and Out of the Apple
Homing

For children

Once There Were Dragons
Boo to a Goose
The Mad Parrot's Countdown
Catching the Spider
The Conjuror's Rabbit

Criticism

Passing Judgements

Depending on the Light

JOHN MOLE

PETERLOO POETS

First published in 1993
by Peterloo Poets
2 Kelly Gardens, Calstock, Cornwall PL18 9SA, U.K.

A catalogue record for this book is available from the British Library

ISBN 1-871471-38-9

Printed in Great Britain by
Latimer Trend & Company Ltd, Plymouth

ACKNOWLEDGEMENTS: some of the poems in this volume have apppeared in the following publications: *Agenda, The Cambridge Review, The Critical Quarterly, The Critical Survey, Encounter, First and Always* (edited by Lawrence Sail, Faber & Faber, 1988), *The Independent on Sunday, The London Magazine, The Observer, Outposts, Owl, Poetry and Audience, Poetry Book Society Anthology 1* (edited by Fraser Steel, Hutchinson, 1990), *The Poetry Review, PN Review, The Rialto, The Spectator, The Times Literary Supplement, The Times Saturday Review.*

Supported by

for Peter Goodden

Contents

The Cherry Tree

Welcome to the cherry,
So unequivocal,
So full
Of itself, so utterly

Not you, not me, with our same
Questions,
The old stones'
Word game

Of this year
Last year
Next year
Never…

Of *Do you love me*
As much as…?
Or *Who was*
He or she?

Or *Do you love me less*
Than I love you?
Or *Tell me something new.*
Haven't I heard this?

Welcome to the cherry,
Its white silence,
Its common sense,
Its letting be.

A Dream of Bed-Time

Often they'd stand beside the yarrow
In their yard, the clustering flat-topped
Bunch of it, the yearning yellow

Taller than them both, much taller
Than her son who'd clutch at a single stem
And bend it, face to face. He'd watch her

Watching him, that sidelong glance
At each of them, that dressing-gown
An even brighter yellow, but not innocence

Or childish candour, more a complicity
Which sometimes let the stem bend back and sometimes
Snapped the head off, asking *Do you really love me?*

The House by the Railroad

The theatre of incompatibility
Is Gothic, always a final scene
Unscripted, and its backdrop
Just such a house as this, a stuccoed
Shadow-box, a crepuscule
Of far too many windows
Facing everywhere. *If he had only seen*
What I can ... how it might have been
The morning they first woke together, light's
Accomplices, returning to that tall bed
Warm and gilded with their night things
Rustling on the quilt as if alive
And as they left them ... *Now*
Even to hear his voice is terrible, to wake
Outside, to snatch the joker
From this house of cards, to lay him on the line
Face-down and sleep alone
Until the midnight wheels pass over;
Or until the birds that sang on
Staves of silver wire, love's telegraph,
Lift off, diminuendo, darkening
To specks of omen, only one of them
Returning with a different song
To pause a moment, weightless in the air,
Then touch down on the house to topple it.

The Falling Man

And finally, the act
We'd waited for,
Our own inimitable
Falling Man

Who climbed his pyramid
Of chairs and tables
With a whimper
And a sheepish grin

Until, so nearly there,
He cried out, leaping
From a crumpled clatter
Clear into the stalls

Where all of us
Applauded, rushed to be
The one who set him on his feet
And brushed him down

While brisk assistants
Rearranged the stage,
Rebuilt the whole construction
Higher still, more skeletal,

And so, prepared,
He turned again to bow
Then set off warmed
By fresh applause

Which chilled to silence
As he neared the top
And this time
Would he by a whisker

Make it? No,
But as he fell
How irreversibly his mirth
Became our guilt

And as he lay there
In that wooden cage
Collapsed around him
Laughing, laughing

At our laughter,
It was you that cried out
Look, The Falling Man has fallen,
Help him. Help!

Travellers

The pin-striped thug, the middle-aged
Sartorial bully is a lost soul
In this tunnel. Tense, ophthalmic
On the edge of murder, going
Nowhere between stations. Opposite
I read a book and then pretend to, watching
As his anger swells from silence,
Pours into a well that can't contain it
And the black bile overflows. A girl
Sits down beside him opening her bag
And taking out three carrots. She begins
To bite them—click, click, click, click—
As if he wasn't there, as if beside her
Was a gentleman who wouldn't mind
Because he was a gentleman, at most
Might be amused by this—click, click—
Or say *My little rabbit*, but instead
His sour face swivels round towards her
Muttering *More noise, come on, please*
Make more noise, why not, let's hear it,
We all want to hear it! He attempts
A supercilious snarl. Her pale face
Pales still further but her eyes are tip-toe
On the edge of murder. She outfaces him,
She blinks, she bites again—click, click—
And gazes coldly. She will never be
His victim but again he tries. *If you don't*
Stop I'll pull the communication cord
And then you'll have to and that won't
Be all—click, click, click, click,
She finishes. She reaches for another. *Do*
She says *then you'll be fined*—click, click—
Until he sits there speechless and until
I close my book. The train slows down. She says
I think there's something wrong with you …
I leave at the next station.

Song of the Double Pay-Out

'Cash if you die. Cash if you don't.'
Insurance Company Slogan.

The watchdog tracks
Its ticking eye
Across the likes
Of you and me;
The agent's key
Should fit, but won't.
Love if you die,
Love if you don't.

The dealer stacks
The cards too high
For simple luck's
Hot property;
Connubial we
Should win, but won't.
Love if you die,
Love if you don't.

The future lacks
The heart to lie
And tries to fix
What it can't see;
Leaves to the tree
Should come but won't.
Love if you die,
Love if you don't.

The outcome packs
Its bags to fly
From passion's complex
Unity;
Doubtless we
Should too, but won't.
Love if you die,
Love if you don't.

The Edward Lear Poem

He kept his wife in a box he did
And she never complained though the neighbours did
Because of the size of the box and the way
He tried to behave in a neighbourly way
But smiled too much of a satisfied smile
For a body to know what to make of his smile.

Then there came such a terrible cry one night
Of the kind you don't like to hear in the night
Though the silence that followed was broken at last
By the blows of a hammer which seemed to last
For ever and ever and ever and ever
And no-one set eyes on that man again ever.

La Jeunesse

Straight from her door
Through rows of vines towards
The river, one white bucket
Swinging for Sunday, the air
Fleshed out with heat
So plump this risen morning
Purpling to ripeness
But not yet, but not quite
Yet among these sunflowers
Leaning their weary faces
Huge and vacant
After her, so stooped
So nodding, and the one
Note tolling distantly
Across the river *mort*
La mort comme ça aussi la mort
From the little church's
Bell tower on a low hill
Rising from the vines
And ringing, swinging
Its one black upturned
Bucket emptying
All gathered sound this morning
Everywhere *la vie la mort*
Although she has turned already
Walking to her door.

To His Love, Sleeping

(Jules Supervielle: *La Dormeuse*)

Because when faces close
They still converse
In questions and answers
Beneath their repose
And because you are two
With the one face
Doubly wise
And just as true
When, sleeping, your eyes
So sweetly abscond
To a country beyond
Their lids as they fall
Or when they return
To the world that we call
Ours with its clouds, trees,
Its palpable mysteries,
I shall never know
Enough of truth
To choose either or both—
The light of your eyes
On this life we are given
Or that secretive glow
Behind shut lids
Where you wait, hidden.

The Settlement

Steam from an electric kettle
Shrouds its click, then
Two cerulean mugs across the lawn
This droughty summer
Come as a libation
Weighted, brimming, answering
The love which reaches
Out for them, still reaching
For the girl who held them
Balanced just the same
Though in a greener garden
Twenty years ago, held now
Against their soon becoming
Shards discovered in a dry bed
Dusted over.

Shrouded too
But by blue dazzle, light years
From such thoughts as these,
Imperious, perching
On the terra-cotta chimney
Rising from gold thatch,
A gull there briefly
Lifts its Roman head.

The Honesty Box

Bolt upright, seated in a ring
They played the game again
Like ancient children. Not a sound,
No music, not the rustling
Of tissue, nothing that began
Or seemed that it could ever
Stop. And so the box came round
As it had always done, a heavy-hearted
Dull exchange, a passing-on
Of what was neither grief
Nor fear nor hope but only
Mere deception. Some
Gazed blankly at it, some
Were rid of it without a glance
And just a few occasionally
Held it up to listen, hearing
Locked inside the key
Which might have opened it at last,
A distant rattle.

Then, as they
Shifted it like this from lap
To lap, the miracle occurred. Some
Smiled a little and some wept,
Each cautious, quivering lip
A voice which in another world
Was coming clean, no longer
Guilty of its secret, opening
What one by one these held
In common yet had never spoken of
Until this moment when it seemed
A huge lid lifted from the room
Releasing kindness like a breath
Of sandalwood, so suddenly, so
Sweetly from this box they'd all
Been lost in, as their vision
Gave them to each other, as the key
Turned once in silence and was gone.

The Loop

Again as he came to bed
It rained, the hiss
Of another day's
Remorse recorded, played there
In the dark—

A curtain beyond the curtains
And beyond that
Voices, his and hers,
Repeating every last thought
Left unspoken

Or the shroud which all day
Wrapped their silence,
The sheer
Drench of attrition,
A sentence without words …

Tomorrow she'd say
It's raining when she woke
And nothing more, and he
It was when I came to bed
In mere continuation

Of that same looped tape,
Its steady silence
Still too deep for tears
Or any tenderness to wipe them—

A life soaked to the skin.

When

When, around 5 a.m., she turns
And sighs with what is never now
Sweet shifting between dreams, a murmurous
Adjustment of her pillow, but
Familiar despair, his cue
To ask *Are you still awake?* and hers
To utter from a depth
He cannot enter *Yes, I haven't slept,*
Have you?, each thinks it is like

When the dead awake
To find it true this time
Despite their lying accidentally
Beside each other and by habit almost
In each other's arms, as warm
As the residual ash
Of love or anger, wondering
If anything at all then why they are
Here unpuzzled by the dawn's
Irresolution, not ashamed
As once they might have been
By what is brought to light.

A Different Dream

Here is the place for them, the fathers
Who were children, in this clearing
Ringed with cypresses, a garden
Where their love of it can cut the grass
Forever, and the house we all remember
Casts no shadow on the lawn. It's here
In a dream I meet with mine again, his sleeves
Rolled up for the honest work
Just asking to be done. He says
I'll need some help. His tie
Is tucked inside his waist-band, braces
Tight and at the ready. Go!
I walk beside him with a little barrow
As my mother watches us a while
And then goes in. This is the place for us
Until the light starts fading:
Cold my father says *It's turning cold*—
We look up, and a cloud is hanging there
Above the cypresses. We're in
A different dream, a darker.

Now we stand beside each other, loving, lost
And very tired. He says
We've done it, leaning on the mower
At our completed lawn's
Far edge. He calls my mother—*Mother!*—
But she doesn't hear him, no,
Not even as he snaps his braces
In the slack and stoop of weariness.
By now she's reading the illuminated text
Of sunset from a western window
In her empty house: **God blesses**
Those who bless themselves
And then it's over. This is her love's
Last frame. I'm caught inside it calling

Father! as I run to him again
Across the lawn, beyond my life,
My wife, our children, yes,
For a moment as the two of us
Look once towards the house
Then disappear between the cypresses.

The Journey Back

The journey back is commonplace.
There never was a pedal car
That did not speed across cut grass.

Never was grass that did not grow
Or treasure trove without its loss
Or knowledge less than all you know.

But never deny the empty street,
The stepping stones you came to cross,
The blank space where all shadows meet,

Where, speeding past you, straight ahead
And driverless, a pedal car
Returns as if to beat the dead.

The Walking Bell

(after Goethe)

Once there was a Sunday child
Who would not go to church,
Who ran into a sunlit field
As far as he could reach.

His mother warned him *Hear the bell!*
You must not make it wait.
Unless you heed the good Lord's call
That bell will seek you out.

No! cried the Sunday child, *Not so,*
It cannot leave its tower.
So off without a care he flew.
He'd darken no priest's door.

And now the bell no longer tolled.
So much for mother's tales.
But what was this? The Sunday child
Turned on his troubled heels.

The bell was chasing after him,
An angry, brazen dome,
It waddled like that scourge of sin
The pastor, crying *Come,*

There's no escape for Sunday's child,
For mother's boy, for you.
You shall forget your sunlit field.
God has decreed it so.

On pumping, pious little legs
With the walking bell behind him,
Torn by briars and lashed by twigs,
The Sunday child ran blindly

Where mother and the pastor stood
To greet him at the porch
And, flanking him on either side,
Escort him into church.

So now, they say, the child is whole
Who'd sickened in the sun
But every time he hears the bell
Virtue goes out of him

And though one stroke, one stroke alone
Can bring him to his knees,
He still recalls the light that shone
Once in a field of praise.

The Carolling Bull

Beware, beware the carolling bull
With its gate wide open, oh three bags full
And over the moon, sing high, sing low,
Sing *Dulce, in dulci jubilo*
With a ring through its nose, a roar in its heart
For everything that's about to start
All over again and again and again
For the little boy who lives down the lane,
Who sleeps on straw then stirs and cries
And remembers how once before his eyes
The stable door burst open wide
As, full of a rush of headlong pride,
It thundered out, the carolling bull,
By Jove, by Jehovah, a holy fool
High on an overdose of joy
And love and rage for its own sweet boy
Who had woken from a dream of peace
To weep at this terrible release,
This sudden, glorious weight of a world
Which would not grow wise but simply old
In a field of praise, still standing there,
The carolling bull, beware, beware.

In All Things

Singing *Teach me my God*
And King, you swept
The same room over and over
For his laws,

For the God of brooms
And dusters who shall see
Himself in the polished table
Face to face.

Prayer was the breath
Which misted silver
As you buffed it up
Then saw him shine

Or when he answered
In excelsis
From the firmament
Of thrumming wires.

Bent at the fireplace
Which we named your altar
With its two brass candle-sticks
And marbled clock

Oh the bone in my leg
You muttered, rising
I'd rather wear out, though,
Than rust out,

And you did, a home help
Humming the Beatles
Paid by the hour
To sweep around your feet.

The Family Friend

Each year, those eyes
Ablaze with temperance
And love for all of us
Above the rim, she
Held it out, her glass's
Fluted blossom, pinch-me-tightly
Plucking at its stem
Although she'd *never normally*
But just this once
Because of Christmas, planting it
Beside my father's plate.

And he, that cloudy frown
Of mock-reproof
So solemnly disguising
Mischief's kindliness, would
Raise the bottle high, a patriarchal
Grand parabola to shower
Celestial liquor, then
Dip suddenly depositing
A little drop, permissible
And blessed by silence
As it passed her lips.

Passing the Parcel

While the music was playing she passed him the parcel
And he passed it back to her slowly at first
As if guessing its weight or perhaps just admiring
The shop-window gloss of its polka-dot wrapping
But faster then faster they thrust it between them
Away and away like a short-fused explosive.

Until it was there in his hands and no music
Which meant that he had to begin to unwrap it
By layer and layer and layer and layer
But he took his time and she wasn't watching
As if they had somehow decided already
The party was over and nothing was in it.

No Answer

They watched his indiscretion
Then arrested him.

They will not name it,
What he did.

With just six words
They broke him—

In their report they wrote
We stood at a respectable distance.

What is a life
According to that measurement?

How far the distance
Worthy of respect?

Item

She left it in the long grass
Bedded there, lullay lullay,
And started walking, anywhere, away
Across a world of darkness to the edge

Then stopped forever, come what may
Of any reckoning. What came to pass
Was boots and tracker dogs, a village
Briefly on the news, the interviews

With nobody who loved her
But must say so anyway, much outrage,
Not a little pity, and rejoicing
For the child found sleeping where it lay.

The Innocents

Two candles on a cake
And blown out in one breath
Are all they need to take
The mortal sting from death,

To reassure them both
That love is safe and sound,
That constant shoots of growth
Still spring up from a ground

Which being theirs on trust
Seems certain to endure
Because they know it must
Although they can't be sure,

Although a cruel death
Which reason won't explain
Blew out in one breath
All innocence from pain

And left this tiny corpse
Beside the railway track,
So truth must take its course—

There is no turning back.

Lovely

What he most cares for now
Are oranges (beside his bed
The jordan, sweetly sour,
Afloat with curlicues of peel
Like Chinese lanterns
Drifting there beneath
Stained fingers and the smack
Of restless lips)

And chocolates, spilling
Sticky centres in a cataract
Through stubble from a source still
Mortally Olympian, the baffled
Godhead, whining *Lovely,*
Lovely, lovely...

The Waking

Nothing, it seems, not crowded out
By war, and in my sleep
Its rumours, pad-foot, prowling
Through the darkness dreams
Are guilty of, as if each touch
Were breaking sanctions, love
Reported somewhere culpable
In snow or sandstorm, ambushed
And arraigned with you
Beside me as we walk there
In whatever place is sacred to
The guilt of happiness
Towards a daybreak smeared
Across the blank horizon
Of a barred world, curtainless
And shadowing our bed.

Yet still, without shame,
A place for this, the waking
To familiar warmth, the slow
Shift over of your body
To the groove my rising's
Left for it, the loosed
Indulgent yawn along
The length of you, and arms
Stretched up beyond the headboard
With a little moan, a sensual
Smile by Rembrandt or Vermeer
Or, should you choose, Matisse
Depending on the light
And then the coffee waiting
And the first cars
Coughing in the street.

The Installation

En route for coastal
Sea and sand,
Do we dream
This hinterland

Where, cordoned-off
And disenchanted,
A curious garden
Has been planted?

Though it lies here
In the light
Everything seems
Dead of night.

Someone guards
A little hut
Whose door is barred
And windows shut.

Mottled cars
Speed to and fro
On runways
Where we must not go.

Revolving turrets'
Moony plates
Protect a world
Which waits and waits.

A skull-and-crossbones
On live wire
Proclaims its voltage
Like desire.

A lonely golfer
Plays his shot,
Making the place
Seem what it's not.

An innocent
Ballistic sphere
Leaps from the dust
To disappear.

At the crash gates
Men with guns
Scuff their boots
And bite their thumbs.

While, troubled by
The watch they keep,
We neither wake
Nor dare to sleep.

Land's End

Now, having reached this point,
What is it? Rocks,
Rocks, rocks, rocks,
The sea's ambiguous answer.

The Point

was not where it went
but where it led him,
how he found it
in the music, out of it
and back, each chorus
risking more, the changes
unrepeatable, already
way beyond transcription
like his wide-mouthed
braying laughter, bracelet
slung on each wrist, percussive
signet fingers, then
that grin and all he'd
ever tell them: *Sure it's dangerous*
And when you see me smiling
You know I'm lost.

Benny Goodman

Studying the dance-floor
Through a scholar's glasses,
Soul of strict measure
And precise notation —

Running wild,
His cool quicksilver
Head arrangements
Darted into place,

Or flying home
In a white tuxedo
With the boys behind him
And the heat turned on

He came and conquered,
Little Caesar,
Colonising jazz
From town to town

And so to Moscow
Where the iron curtain
Rose for him
Although *With Benny*

Every gig (a sideman said)
Was like playing in Russia,
Swing on the rocks,
A counterpoint of ice.

Stan Laurel

Ollie gone, the heavyweight
Balletic chump, and now
His turn to bow out, courteous,
A perfect gentleman who
Tips his hat to the nurse

Or would, that is, if he were
Still in business. She
Adjusts his pillow, smooths
The sheets until their crisp-
And-even snow-white starchiness

Becomes his cue. It's time
For one last gag, the stand-up
Drip-feed: *Sister,*
Let me tell you this,
I wish I was skiing,

And she, immaculately cornered
For the punch-line: *Really,*
Mr Laurel, do you ski? A chuckle —
No, but I'd rather I was doing
That than this,

Than facing death, the one
Fine mess he's gotten into
That he can't get out of
Though a nurse's helpless laughter
Is the last he hears.

Dream Girl

I was the girl who wrote to Noël Coward,
Dated Errol Flynn and Edward G.,
Stiffened her upper lip for Leslie Howard,
Brought Clark Gable down on bended knee,
Drove around the block with Fred MacMurray,
Rode the Ferris Wheel with Orson Welles,
Told the Hays Committee not to worry,
Promised Walter Pidgeon wedding bells,
Followed Bogey's hat down every mean street,
Shared Paul Henreid's last two cigarettes,
Tried in vain to fathom Sidney Greenstreet,
Settled George Raft's hash by placing bets …
I was the girl who nearly lost her head
But fell asleep and married you instead.

Poetry Now

To celebrate the return of Radio 3's programme, two senior poets release the poems they wrote in 1985 when they learned that it was to be discontinued.

EH?

He said: Take back your typescripts
creatures. Scribble away
in the silence which is the process
of the absence of the producer
of programmes.
                    Adjust
your sets to the infrequency
of verse, the time's virus
wiping its bacilli
from tangled spools.
                    The lift door
closes with the terminal
susurrus of suspended
operations. It ascends
to that vacancy where you must
shape alone the ultimate
meaning's primal echo
in the studio of the spirit.

TRIADS

I open up a deck-chair on the patio
And think that if poetry is so much crazy paving
Henry James would have seen a pattern in these stones.

Beyond me on the lawn two sparrows quarrel
As I watch them. Then I remember Yeats
Who said that poetry is our quarrel with ourselves.

Yeats was quite a clever chap, and so was Brahms
Who wrote his first symphony when he was over forty.
All the same, I'm sorry *Poetry Now* has gone.

It filled the gaps on Radio Three
(Once called the Third in happier days) reminding us
We cannot all be Brahms or, for that matter, Yeats.

Not that these triads are entirely bosh,
But when I take note of my avian chums
I wonder at the hubris of our pecking order.

Note: *Since these poems were written,* Poetry Now *has, it would appear, been terminally discontinued; and the author of* Triads *died in 1991.*

Train Landscape, 1939

(Eric Ravilious)

Distant and chalk-white horse of innocent
Prehistory, viewed from the left-hand window
In this water-colour of an empty
Third-class carriage pausing
Deep and leisurely in
Little England, there is no-one
Left in the frame now
To regard you but the painter's

Ghost and those of us perhaps
Who might have wished
Just one companion to be journeying
With history's closer, less
Enchanted end in view, just one
Who could not hope to change his fate
For such nostalgia, stop
To gaze at you and then pass on
To yet another picture.

Primary

and there
the space   and here

the choice
of every shade

of all
the colours

blazing
to begin

and here
the red   and there

the blue
and Monsieur Matisse

do you
believe in

God? Yes
when I'm working

The Island Hut

Jaunty, scalloped thinking-cap
Of corrugated iron, pearly
Oyster-coloured off-the-map
Retreat for a poet waking early.

Watchful between wave and stone,
Outcrop outpost, lichen-crusted
Shell of the need to be alone
From day to day uninterrupted.

Ringed lobe of the island's ear,
A heart attentive, tongue-tied speech,
That little vessel always there
Lost in its thought just out of reach.

The Floral Costumier

Open his scented
wardrobe, find
the little silken
arum lilies.

From their green
hangers they
drift towards you
blowing kisses.

Theirs is the soft
sift of a nightdress
in its snowfall
to your ankles

or the sweetness
rising, moist
and downy between
lip and lip.

They are his fingers'
dream of nakedness
made flesh,
an incarnation

of their touch
from root to blossom,
love's amazement
and a perfect fit.

An Indian Miniature

Two lions, though
Not yet a pair,
By half and half
Keep meeting here

Within this frame
Which holds them still
Like thought becoming
Visible

As if at any
Moment they
Might both forget
To walk away

More suddenly
Than either one
Last time, perhaps,
Forgot to come

Since neither guesses
How or why
The other acts
So curiously

Or just what secret
Shares the honours
Between their tails'
Inverted commas.

The Safe Nursery

Never to touch the gold key on the mantelpiece
Never to sharpen a sweet tooth for gingerbread
Never to fall for a promise of palaces
Never to bite on a waxed apple's shininess
Never to tangle with overgrown undergrowth
Never to trust that a beast will negotiate

Always to sniff at the meal put in front of you
Always to listen with caution to grandmother
Always to count up the guests at a Christening
Always to walk out on talkative animals
Always to steer clear of picturesque cottages
Always to make your own bed and then lie on it

The Christmas Angel

Spy of a special branch,
The Christmas angel
Weighs his intelligence
And finds it wanting.

He can scarcely believe
What the little birds tell him
Of an open secret
Not to be kept,

Of love's round-robin
Sealed and delivered
To every doorstep
By a child's pierced hand.

So he spreads the word—
As if, as if—
Like a hush-hush cradle
Rocked in its tree.

The Love-Light

Balanced in our hall-way
On the kitchen chair
I'd brought him, each year
Weightier, more anxiously
Precarious, laughing less
And long about it, he would
Hang the mistletoe, its points
Of pearly love-light, fixing them
Then stepping down, unbending
With a sigh of *Not so young now*
Straightening up again
To the familiar height of
Father where he should be, both feet
Firmly on the ground and calling
All of us — myself already there
But mother first — to
Try it out, he'd say
His arms around us, each year
Tighter, a more precious
Keeping, then last thing
To wind the clock, reminding us
It's getting late and all there was
To do tomorrow.

The Present

He stepped into the room, permitted,
Seen, not heard. His father stood
With glass in hand but sober-suited:
Mother, has the boy been good?

I think he has. Her voice came faintly
From the long sofa where she sat
Between the aunt no-one called Auntie
And the uncle who'd seen to that.

So, he shall have his present. Something
Rustled in a dark recess
Then silence, and then whispering,
Then sudden light, then there it was —

The rocking horse, magnificent,
With stirrups, reins, a crimson bow
Tied round the saddle — heaven-sent
To prove the love they could not show.

He took one step, then dared another,
Folded his hands and bowed his head:
Thank you father. Thank you mother.
Thank you. That was all he said.

The Toy Box

This was what you sat on
In the empty playroom
And pretended not to mind
That no-one missed you.

This was the cell block
At the floor's cold centre,
Isolation's focus
And your bitter throne.

This was the island
Where you hunched in exile,
Emperor of nowhere
But a sea of lino.

This was the loneliness
You still remember
Though you smile at parties
And, of course, join in.

Wind-Up

Gagged on silence, with a look
Of terror in its little eyes,
The clockwork bird has lost its song
And cannot find out what went wrong
However hard it tries.

Broken-hearted, half-way through
The triumph of a gorgeous trill—
The universe seemed filled with sound
Then something juddered, thumped, unwound
And suddenly stopped still.

What a shame. It worked last year.
A Christmas bird should always sing.
Indeed it should, but so life goes
With all our bright arpeggios
Dependent on a spring,

And there it looks down from its branch
With empty throat and beak ajar
While underneath the glittering tree
A child who might have once been me
Winds up his brand new car.

From Start to Finish

Whenever the phone rang she'd already be there
To picture him anxiously dialling her number
Then lifting a finger to scratch at his eyebrow
Or whipping the tangled-up cord like a lariat
And always she'd make herself count ten before the
Colliding hullos then the pause then the love-talk,

But now the slow cell-walk to lift the receiver
To balance it seesaw a rib on her shoulder
To clamp down an ear as she flipped the address book
And searched for a number he claimed he'd forgotten
Then found it and gave it and while he kept chattering
Doodled his face which she almost remembered.

The Mermaid

Beached, grounded, on the rocks,
Up-ended, barnacled, and shivering
Your timbers, swim away with me
From here, become the song I sing
As old as you would have it be
Or young as you remember.

I am whatever wished-for company
You welcome now, the radiance
Of risk or mere serenity,
And offer you this choice, this chance,
This last pure draught of miraculous water.

There are no clocks in the sea.

Not About Roses

(to Mary)

I have never written
A poem about roses,
Supposing them
The thorniest subject—

How many before me
Have pricked their fingers
On what they thought
Was the only flower,

The one for love
Without really trying
Like the easiest word
To understand

Or a rhyme so exact
It would live for ever
In its cut-glass bowl
And not need water.

Harder than that
To say *I love you*
With the words still earthed
In a dusty soil

Which nevertheless
Is best for sunflowers
Though too dry for me
To do you justice

Or offer more
Than the curious drift
Of a loving poem
Not about roses.

Revenant

Under our bedroom window
Held by memory between
The full moon and the high wall's
Shadow, a familiar
Hooped barrel on its makeshift
Rickety pram-wheeled
Wooden trolley as we
Throw the shutters open after
Loving on the old
Low bolstered bed and
In the dark no longer, held
By this moment only
And the silent tenderly
Yearning upward of that same
Still single-fruited
Moonlit lemon tree.

Sketching the Tortoise

Sketching the tortoise
should be easy, eye

To unblinking eye
with post-diluvian pencilled

fingers, but it isn't, shifting
ceaselessly like

wind through grass or
fidgeting those

little eucalyptus leaves
from light to shade

to light, so slight
you scarcely notice what

it's up to, what
it almost tells us

not of ourselves alone
but of imagination's

origins, the slowness
of a patient world

revealed by everything
which won't keep still.

Heavenly

The maximum capacity
However many of our chins
Will fit on other shoulders
In this overloaded
Elevator going up.

Stand clear of the doors
Which shudder to a close
Before the whole box
Trembles and the sky-bound
Ribbed floor rises.

Mine, as it happens,
Is the oldest chin
To settle on the youngest
Shoulder, and my beard
Starts tickling her neck.

She smiles, but this
Is not romantic. This is
What I've always feared—
To be the gentleman, the dull,
Respectable, absurdly

Reassuring circumstance
Where decency controls. A voice
Cries *Let me out, for pity*
Let me out!, but no-one hears
Because it's only mine

And anyway the doors
Have opened on the upper level
Of an afterlife where angels
In their maximum capacity
Are fitted to each other's arms.

Going On

Scotch and water, warm,
Medicinal, two tablets
On a little tray, his *Times*
Tucked underarm, a dignified
But frail ascent, prolonged
Undressing measured out
By heavy footsteps, coughing
Gently not to worry us, as if
A mere polite reminder, then
The silence of the grave.

And why must I recall this now
As half-way up the stairs
I hear my grown son calling
Going on, then, Dad?
An early night? Sleep well.